CHRIST IN YOU

+

GROUP GUIDE

CHRIST IN YOU

+

WHY GOD TRUSTS YOU MORE THAN YOU TRUST YOURSELF

ERIC JOHNSON

Chosen

a division of Baker Publishing Group
Minneapolis, Minnesota

Published by Chosen Books
11400 Hampshire Avenue South
Bloomington, Minnesota 55438
www.chosenbooks.com

Chosen Books is a division of
Baker Publishing Group, Grand Rapids, Michigan

Printed in the United States of America

ISBN 978-0-8007-9841-3

Cover design by Amy Miller and Brianna Ailie

16 17 18 19 20 21 22   7 6 5 4 3 2 1

Contents

Introduction
Setting the Stage

Welcome to the *Christ in You Group Guide*. This guide will equip you with the knowledge and tools you need to lead a group through the *Christ in You* curriculum.

The *Christ in You* curriculum encapsulates the key ideas of Eric Johnson's book *Christ in You* and invites group participants to apply and activate these concepts through discussion, meditation, study, prayer and various activities. The curriculum includes this group leader guide and six video segments for you to show in a group setting. In the videos, Eric explains and expands on his teaching in the book. Ideally, the curriculum also includes copies of *Christ in You* for each participant. Participants who have not read the book will still be able to engage in the group discussion and activities, but they will have a deeper experience if they read along in the book.

You and your group can complete each of the six sessions in the curriculum in 60 to 90 minutes. As the leader, you will also want to spend a little extra time preparing yourself before each group meeting. Each session is designed with the following format:

- Prepare (for leaders only, ahead of time)
  - Watch Video & Review Notes
  - Think & Write
- Lead (for your group sessions)
  1. Welcome & Key Verse
  2. Session Video
  3. Conversation
  4. Activity
  5. Homework
  6. Prayer

PREPARATION

Before you lead a group through the curriculum, familiarize yourself with this guide to get a sense of the whole journey you will be undertaking with your group. Before you lead each group meeting, take plenty of time to go through the preparation materials in the "Prepare" section of each session. You will want to watch each session video ahead of time and review the quotes taken from Eric's main points in the video. It is also a good idea to read the book chapters that go along with the session and write down some of your thoughts on the material Eric presents. Note-taking space is provided for you.

ACTIVITIES

Each session offers a selection of activities for you and your group. You can complete some of these exercises during the session, while others involve off-site activities that you will need to plan in advance. You may want to plan your six (or more) activities before you start the curriculum, and then be ready to notify your group at each meeting about what they will want to prepare or bring as part of their homework for the next time.

CUE CARDS

To give you greater freedom in leading each session, this guide comes with a set of cue cards at the back that you can remove and use. As you read from the cards, they will guide you through each item in the group session format.

SESSION 1
MINDSETS

For centuries, the Church has largely focused on salvation. The main thrust has been to get people saved so they could go to heaven. What is interesting is that while the Church has spent most of its time talking about going to heaven, Jesus spent quite a bit of His time talking about bringing the Kingdom of heaven to earth.

Christ in You, page 20

PREPARE

Watch Video & Review Notes

(Note that this first session includes a short Introduction video, along with the Session 1 video and the notes that follow.)

1. MINDSET SHIFT

- "For me, one of the greatest master keys of the Kingdom is to realize I am a child of a really good Dad."

- "I got a deeper understanding of how I was viewing the way God thinks of me, God's view of humanity, and His perspective and values. When I began to change these mindsets, it felt as if Colossians 1:27, *Christ in us*, just came alive all over again. I went from *I'm going to heaven someday*, to asking, *What about until I go to heaven?*"

2. GOSPEL OF SALVATION TO GOSPEL OF THE KINGDOM

- "*Christ in us* isn't just about getting saved and going to heaven; it's about seeing His Kingdom come."

- "Salvation means to save, set free, heal and deliver. What I want to unpack is the *expression* of salvation. . . . When we live our lives, we are actually expressing what He has done in us and through us. That is what I am passionate about—seeing the Body of Christ express their salvation and the Kingdom coming to this earth, and seeing it touch every part of our lives and every part of the world we live in."

3. THE MIND OF CHRIST

- "What we ultimately want is to be just like Jesus. A big part of that process is to think how He thinks. How did He view the world? How did He view life?"

- "If my thoughts are not like God's thoughts, if I am not thinking like Jesus, I am going to look at the stuff around me—the Bible, you, the world around us—with a dirty lens. . . . I am really passionate about us renewing our thinking and mindsets, because the lens becomes Christlike and we begin to actually live a life the way Jesus did."

4. OUR ASSIGNMENT

- "What is at stake for us (if we don't renew our minds) is that we truly won't see the Kingdom come. Jesus actually gave that assignment to us to see the Kingdom come. . . . I think we lose our purpose, our destiny—everything in some ways."

- "The idea of this book and my heart really is that people would have permission to go higher. . . . I would love for us to have the heart of a child . . . and have the desire to jump higher and the permission to climb higher."

- "I want to become like Jesus, and I want to see the Body of Christ become more like Jesus, where we see every part of society touched by Jesus and see His Kingdom come. I pray that we would actually fall in love with Jesus all over again . . . and realize that the greatest Person ever is actually living inside us."

ADDITIONAL NOTES:

_____

_____

_____

_____

_____

_____

_____

_____

_____

_____

THINK & WRITE

"Session 1: Mindsets" introduces the idea that Christians need to shift their mindset away from thinking about the Christian life primarily as something that happened in the past—getting saved—and something that will happen in the future—going to heaven. Eric covers this in the Introduction and chapters 1 and 2 of the book, which you will want to read before leading your group. This session raises the following questions:

- What is life supposed to be like on the other side of the cross, inside the Kingdom?
- How are we expressing our "salvation" in our day-to-day lives?
- Do we really think about ourselves the way God thinks about us?
- Do we live with permission to go "higher" in our pursuit of becoming like Jesus and seeing His Kingdom come in and through us?

Before leading Session 1, spend some time meditating on these questions. Write down two or three thoughts, experiences and insights from your life that you can share with the group.

_____

_____

_____

_____

_____

_____

_____

WHAT YOU WILL NEED

- Introduction video, Session 1 video
- Pens and paper if you choose to do Activity 1

LEAD

1. WELCOME & KEY VERSE (SEE CUE CARD)

Welcome your group to the *Christ in You* curriculum. Take a minute at the very beginning of this first session to show the Introduction video. Then read (or have someone in the group read) the Key Verse twice:

> But the natural man does not receive the things of the Spirit of God, for they are foolishness to him; nor can he know them, because they are spiritually discerned. But he who is spiritual judges all things, yet he himself is rightly judged by no one. For "who has known the mind of the LORD that he may instruct Him?" But we have the mind of Christ.
>
> 1 Corinthians 2:14–16

Ask the group, "What sticks out to you in these verses? How do they apply to your life?" Allow two or three people to respond.

2. SESSION VIDEO

Watch the Session 1 video.

3. CONVERSATION (CUE CARD)

Share one or two thoughts from your preparation work, and then discuss the following:

- What does it mean to think of yourself as the child of a really good Dad? Do we really think about ourselves the way God thinks about us?

- In his introduction to *Christ in You*, Eric writes, "For centuries, the Church has largely focused on salvation. The main thrust has been to get people saved so they could go to heaven. What is interesting is that while the Church has spent most of its time talking about going to heaven, Jesus spent quite a bit of His time talking about bringing the Kingdom of heaven to earth" (page 20). What are the implications of shifting from a "getting saved and going to heaven" mindset to an "expressing salvation now and bringing heaven to earth" mindset?

- What are some ways that we express our salvation and/or see the Kingdom coming as a present reality in our daily lives?

- How do you want the six sessions in this study to change your perception of God? What else do you want to get out of these sessions?

4. ACTIVITY (CUE CARD)

Do one or both of these activities with your group:

1. Word/phrase associations to check your beliefs. Read the following phrases to the group. Have participants write down their first reaction. Then discuss their answers. Ask, "Which phrases didn't feel true?"

   - "God is good."
   - "God trusts you."
   - "You are a saint."
   - "Jesus lives in you."
   - "You were created for great things."

2. Take time to "pull out the gold" in each other. Break up into groups of two or three and encourage each other. Before you speak out, ask God who each person is and what he or she was born for.

5. HOMEWORK (CUE CARD)

Before concluding, encourage each person in the group to do the following before your next session:

- Meditate on 1 Corinthians 2:14–16 throughout the week.
- Ask God what mindset or perceptions He wants to change in you.
- Choose your favorite painting and bring along a print of it next time. Do a little research on the painting so you can tell the group the story behind it. (Leader: Assign this only if the group will be doing Activity 3 next time.)
- If you have a copy of the book *Christ in You*, read the Introduction and chapters 1 and 2 to prepare for the next session.

6. PRAYER (CUE CARD)

Pray this over the group:

Father, we thank You that we are the sons and daughters of a really good Dad. Teach us how to see ourselves the way You see us. Show us what it means to express our salvation in every area of life.

Jesus, we want to see the world the way You see it. Give us the heart of a child to believe that "Christ in us" means we can go higher and further than we can imagine. Let us become like the One who lives in us and fall in love with You more than ever before. Amen.

SESSION 2
HUMANITY

If our theology does not cause us to love humanity more and more, then we need to question our theology.

You should ask yourself these questions: *Is my heart getting harder and more calloused toward people? Or is it becoming more compassionate?* Your goal, and the goal of every believer, should be to grow in compassion and love for people as you mature in your walk with God.

Christ in You, pages 23–24

PREPARE

Watch Video & Review Notes

(This time includes the Session 2 video and the notes that follow.)

1. THE ARTIST'S PERSPECTIVE

- "As I begin to gain God's value for me and for people, I begin to realize that my own perspective on humanity is more influenced by something else other than God's perspective."

- "The artist began to talk about what she was feeling, what she was thinking and her heart behind this piece of art. I went from not being able to stand the painting to thinking it was a beautiful painting, and that I could understand it. I realized that until I had the artist's perspective on the painting, I only had mine."

- "It's easy to love a great person. But if you look at the broad spectrum of humanity, there's a lot of gnarly stuff going on in the world, and that is one of the hardest things for us—to fall in love with something that has some serious issues."

15

- "I want to challenge us to get God's perspective on humanity. If I am not falling more in love with people over the course of my lifetime, I have to change my theology. Because Jesus had the ultimate expression at the end of His life, and that was to give His life for people."

2. CREATED IN GOD'S IMAGE

- "Everything God created, He said is very good. He expressed His value for humanity. Not long after Creation, there was the Fall of man. That took everything off course, but I believe it didn't change God's value for people. It just became a massive wrench in the system."

- "I want to challenge people that we wouldn't see humanity through the eyes of sin, but we would see humanity through the eyes of God. It doesn't disregard sin and say it isn't an issue. It actually reveals the nastiness of sin when you actually see what God had in mind."

- "I am passionate that we would engage society and culture with a value for people. I want to engage with you because I actually love you and I see the way God sees you. I am challenging myself to look at some of the gnarliest people alive today and ask myself if I can find a love for them. I think that is going to enable us as a Body of Christ to see the Great Commission take place."

- "When Jesus died, He paid the greatest price. He paid the greatest price because people have value. I think it is important for us to have that value for people."

3. HIS GOODNESS LEADS TO REPENTANCE

- "I came across this verse in the Bible that talks about how His goodness leads us to repentance; His kindness leads us to repentance (see Romans 2:4). And I said to my team, 'We have too many things aimed at "repent first." We need to flip the script. Our responsibility as leaders and as people is to help people see the goodness of God. . . . I don't want us to tell kids anymore what they can and can't do. . . . Let's just hold their hand and lead them as close to God as possible.'"

- "I would have kids sit down and tell me about what they did last weekend. Inside I was freaking out and thinking, *What are you thinking?* But I wouldn't flinch. Then I would move into trying to show them the goodness of God. Over the next two, three, four years, we saw young person after young person come to Jesus because they were exposed to His goodness."

- "I had to learn that God loves people, and when He reveals Himself to people, the natural response is, 'I can't live this life anymore, and I don't want to live this life anymore. I am unattracted to these things now because I have seen God's love for me.'"

4. LOVE AND TRUTH

- "Ask God to point out attitude mindsets, comments, thoughts that you have toward people that aren't His thoughts. I know the Holy Spirit wants to reveal those. When you interact with someone who made you upset . . . ask God about your attitude toward that person. . . . We are around people all the time, so we have a lot of opportunities to hear God's heart for people."

- "Sometimes I won't meet with someone if my heart is off. I will postpone the meeting until I get my heart and attitude in the right place, because I want to live a life where I am interacting with people from a place of love and not from any other place."

- "Truth is best in the context of love. I think sometimes a lot of believers unfortunately love truth so much, but there is no foundation of love in communicating that truth. Knowing truth is so important, but make sure it is coming from a place of love and not from any other place."

- "Jesus has been reduced to a set of beliefs. I think that is one of the reasons why the Body of Christ is so steeped in truth without love. Our faith may have started out as a relationship, but now it is just a set of beliefs that we live by. We don't actually know Him. So I want to draw the Church back to intimacy and that first love."

- "Engage with people who hate God. Engage with atheists. Engage with people who are bitter, and see where your heart is toward them. I practice when I am watching TV and some celebrity is blowing up their life and the world around them. What is my heart toward them? Instead of criticizing them from my living room couch, I want to find out how God thinks of them."

ADDITIONAL NOTES:

_____

_____

_____

_____

_____

_____

_____

_____

THINK & WRITE

"Session 2: Humanity" challenges us to compare our value for people with God's value for them. In order to see God's value for people, we must view them within the full context of the story of Creation, the Fall, redemption and restoration. Though the Fall marred the image of God in humanity—the original design of the Artist—it has not changed His value for humanity. The overwhelming proof of this is seen in God sending Jesus not only to restore our humanity, but to transform it by permanently joining our natures to His through His death and resurrection.

Aligning our value for people with God's value requires us to adjust the way we approach people. Eric covers this in chapters 1 and 2 of the book, which you already read before leading the first session. He also talks a little in this session about one of his key ideas from chapter 4, being the child of a really good Dad, so you may also want to read ahead in that chapter before leading your group. This session raises the following questions:

- Are we seeking to gain God's perspective on and love for people—especially those we find difficult to love?
- How does seeing the Artist's original design for humanity help us understand the true effects of sin?
- How should Jesus' sacrifice for sinners shape the way we view and interact with people?
- If the goodness of God is what leads to repentance, then how do we need to adjust in order to show people His goodness?
- How do we communicate the truth in love?

Before leading Session 2, spend some time meditating on these questions. Write down two or three thoughts, experiences and insights from your life that you can share with the group.

_____

_____

_____

_____

_____

_____

_____

WHAT YOU WILL NEED

- Session 2 video
- A print of your favorite painting to show the group, along with the story behind it, if you choose to do Activity 3
- Materials/arrangements for any other Activity you have chosen

LEAD

1. WELCOME & KEY VERSE (SEE CUE CARD)

Read (or have someone in the group read) the Key Verse:

Then God said, "Let Us make man in Our image, according to Our likeness; let them have dominion over the fish of the sea, over the birds of the air, and over the cattle, over all the earth and over every creeping thing that creeps on the earth." So God created man in His own image; in the image of God He created him; male and female He created them. Then God blessed them, and God said to them, "Be fruitful and multiply; fill the earth and subdue it; have dominion over the fish of the sea, over the birds of the air, and over every living thing that moves on the earth."

And God said, "See, I have given you every herb that yields seed which is on the face of all the earth, and every tree whose fruit yields seed; to you it shall be for food. Also, to every beast of the earth, to every bird of the air, and to everything that creeps on the earth, in which there is life, I have given every green herb for food"; and it was so. Then God saw everything that He had made, and indeed it was very good. So the evening and the morning were the sixth day.

Genesis 1:26–31

Ask the group, "What sticks out to you in these verses? How do they apply to your life?" Allow two or three people to respond.

2. SESSION VIDEO

Watch the Session 2 video.

3. CONVERSATION (CUE CARD)

Share one or two thoughts from your preparation work, and then discuss the following:

- How can we tell if our hearts are getting harder and more calloused toward people, or are we becoming more compassionate?
- Think of some people you find difficult to love. What does God say about these people (or their group, if applicable)?

- In *Christ in You*, Eric writes, "If we are going to navigate the sin and evil rampant on the earth and help usher the Kingdom into every level of society, we have to recognize how important it is to see the image of God in every person we meet. If we do not realize the importance of that image in them, we most likely will deal with sin and evil from the basis of a short-term mindset that has as its goal alleviating the consequences of sin but not helping the person become healthy and whole as well as saved.

  "I believe that if we as believers have a good grasp of seeing the image of God in people, then we will cultivate a deep love for them that does not have an agenda attached. People will not become the objects of our agenda. Rather, we will see the uniqueness of each person, and we will spend our lives simply loving people into the Kingdom. That all by itself is bound to have an eternal effect on our churches, government and society" (pages 33–34).

  What does it mean to deal with sin with a short-term mindset? What does it mean to love people without having an agenda?

4. ACTIVITY (CUE CARD)

Do any of these activities with your group:

1. Invite someone you would not normally have a meal with to lunch—maybe a sports team coach, a homeless person, a business owner, a neighbor or a pastor. Ask the person, "What's your story?" Show real interest and aim to see who he or she is as a person.
2. Volunteer as a group to help a neighbor or someone in your church. (Ideas: Rake leaves, help a family move, cook dinner for an older couple, etc.)
3. Have everyone talk for a few minutes about the print they brought of their favorite painting, on which they have done a little research so they can share the story behind it.

5. HOMEWORK (CUE CARD)

Before concluding, encourage each person in the group to do the following before your next meeting:

- Pick someone you know or some high-profile person (a celebrity, politician, CEO, etc.) whom you frequently criticize or have a hard time loving. Give God permission to talk to you about your attitude toward that person. Ask Him to change your heart and attitude.
- Bring your favorite gadget or invention with you to the next group session, or a picture of it if the item is too big. (Leader: Assign this only if the group will be doing Activity 1 next time.)

- If you have a copy of the book *Christ in You*, read chapters 3 and 4 to prepare for the next session.

6. PRAYER (CUE CARD)

Pray this over the group:

Father, You made us in Your image. Then You became one of us, died for us and rose again as the image of redeemed humanity. As we look at ourselves and those around us, let us see Your image, Your value and Your love more clearly than anything else. Encounter us with Your goodness, so we can show that goodness to a world full of people whom You love. Amen.

SESSION 3

LIGHT

Can you imagine if each one of us as believers approached the way we spend our time with the idea in mind that everything we do in life is ministry unto the King? We would have fewer believers trying to get into the pulpits to preach and a lot more believers spending more of their time touching the people they live with and interact with every day.

Christ in You, page 70

PREPARE

Watch Video & Review Notes

(This time includes the Session 3 video and the notes that follow.)

1. THE BIBLICAL IMAGERY OF LIGHT

- "In Psalm 67:1–2, King David had this cry: 'God be merciful to us and bless us, and cause His face to shine upon us, that Your way may be known on earth, your salvation among all nations.' David was saying, 'Lord, I want Your favor and Your light to shine on me so when the nations see me in my light, they ask the greatest question—*Who is your God?*' The fruit of that would be that people would come to God by seeing God's light on someone's life."

- "In the New Testament, Jesus says that light is now *in* you, and to let your light shine. So instead of it being an external light shining *on* me, it is an external light shining *from* me. He doesn't say, *Let My light shine*; He says, *Let your light shine*."

- "It's like having a flashlight on all the time. Whether I am in a good mood or not, that light is shining from me. When you begin to unpack this whole idea of light actually living in us and coming from us, it starts to change how we actually engage. Instead of hiding away or being immobile, we are actually being mobile now."

2. MINISTRY AND THE SPIRITUAL

- "For a lot of the Body of Christ, their view of ministry is limited to 'I have to be on staff at a church. I have to be a missionary. I have to preach.' Are all those things ministering? Absolutely. But we aren't confined to just those things. When we begin to realize that the light is actually coming from us, it erases the lines around what is ministry."

- "Ministry is more about who you are. Everything in my life has the potential to be ministry to the King. In Jewish culture, their work was worship to the King. This light is in you so you can work at Starbucks and be in a place of ministry."

- "Some of my favorite testimonies are of people in the church who were trying to get on staff at the church and are now starting a business. They are bringing excellence to our city, wealth and prosperity, and are actually adding strength to a culture and society. . . . There are places in society that church ministers will never have access to. . . . But there are people in our churches and community who are realizing Jesus is shining in them and through them, and everything they do now can be an expression of that light."

- "This conversation about light and erasing lines makes us ask, 'What is spiritual?' My spiritual activities are not just going to church, praying and reading my Bible. Everything I do is spiritual. For me, this is very liberating. If I only view certain things as spiritual, then my wife, kids, finances and everything else I do is kind of second class and not important."

3. WISDOM

- "Proverbs 8 has this great synopsis of Creation. Wisdom says, 'When He marked out the foundations of the earth, then I was beside Him as a master craftsman' (Proverbs 8:29–30). For the Western Church, wisdom has largely been great advice. If you study wisdom more, you find out that wisdom is the creative force in nature. It has the ability to take something worth nothing and make it of value. God did that with Creation—He took something that was void and He made something out of it."

- "When wisdom is in us and on us, it enables us to do things with excellence. It enables us to be creative. It enables us to take something that has no value and make it of value. Wisdom is that one ingredient so essential that we need to go into a neighborhood, city or culture, take something that has lost its value and bring it back to life."

- "Light works best in dark places. The Kingdom is not just about the Church; it's about the world at large—it's about culture, society, humanity. The best thing we can do to find out if we have the light is to get outside the four walls of the church. Get into the places of our city and nation that are void of that and let the light shine and see what happens."

- "Light is the expression of who Jesus is in you. Ephesians 3:10 talks a lot about the believer expressing the manifold wisdom of God, the creativity of God and the intelligence of God. What could that look like? What is that unique thing about you that is Jesus and you together? That is your light—the unique expression of who you are in Him."

ADDITIONAL NOTES:

_____

_____

_____

_____

_____

_____

_____

THINK & WRITE

"Session 3: Light" unpacks the biblical image Jesus used—that we all have *light* within us, which we are not to hide (see Matthew 5:14–16). It is the light of Christ and His Kingdom, and we are to express it—not just in what we typically call "spiritual" activities, but in every aspect of our lives. Because of Christ in us, every human activity is now an opportunity for His light to shine. All of life is spiritual, is worship, is ministry, is Kingdom. In particular, the light of the Kingdom shines through us as we demonstrate God's wisdom and creativity, even in the mundane. Eric covers this in chapter 3 of the book, which you will want to read before leading your group. (Also read chapter 4.) This session raises the following questions:

- How have we been creating false limits around what counts as ministry or spiritual activity?

- What might we be disregarding as a possible expression of our "light" because we are thinking within these limits?

- What are some of the mundane aspects of our lives where we need to tap in to the wisdom and creativity of God?

- Do we really believe that God wants to attract people to the Kingdom through the favor on our lives?

Before leading Session 3, spend some time meditating on these questions. Write down two or three thoughts, experiences and insights from your life that you can share with the group.

_____

_____

_____

_____

_____

_____

_____

_____

WHAT YOU WILL NEED

- Session 3 video

- Pens and paper if you choose to do Activity 2

- One of the themes for this week is that we are a light to attract nations. Change the lighting for your group. Light some candles or hang some twinkly lights to make the lighting more attractive. See if anyone comments on the change.

- If you choose to do Activity 1, remember to bring a gadget or invention for yourself to share with your group, or a picture if the item is too big.

LEAD

1. WELCOME & KEY VERSE (SEE CUE CARD)

Read (or have someone in the group read) the Key Verse:

The LORD possessed me at the beginning of His way, before His works of old. I have been established from everlasting, from the beginning, before there was ever an earth. When there were no depths I was brought forth, when there were no fountains abounding with water. Before the mountains were settled, before the hills, I was brought forth; while as yet He had not made the earth or the fields, or the primal dust of the world. When He prepared the heavens, I was there, when He drew a circle on the face of the deep, when He established the clouds above, when He strengthened the fountains of the deep, when He assigned to the sea its limit, so that the waters would not transgress His command, when He marked out the foundations of the earth, then I was beside Him as a master craftsman; and I was daily His delight, rejoicing always before Him, rejoicing in His inhabited world, and my delight was with the sons of men.

Proverbs 8:22–31

Ask the group, "What sticks out to you in these verses? How do they apply to your life?" Allow two or three people to respond.

2. SESSION VIDEO

Watch the Session 3 video.

3. CONVERSATION (CUE CARD)

Share one or two thoughts from your preparation work, and then discuss the following:

- In *Christ in You*, Eric writes, "David tapped into the heart of God and realized that God wants to bless us abundantly in every area of our lives, to the point that the nations take notice. I believe one of the ways for believers to disciple the nations is to walk out the favor and abundance that God shines in and on our lives" (page 61). Do you feel as if you have tapped in to the heart of God in this way? Why or why not?

- What is spiritual? Are there areas of your life you have viewed as non-spiritual? How would you approach such an area differently if you saw it as worship to God and ministry to others?

- What are some examples of what it looks like to take something of no value and make it of value through the wisdom and creativity of God?

4. ACTIVITY (CUE CARD)

Do any of these activities with your group:

1. Wisdom is not just good advice; it is creativity and problem-solving. Have everyone talk about the gadget or invention they brought. How did it change or improve their lives? How would their lives be different without it? How does this express wisdom?

2. Do another word association exercise with the word *light*. Have everyone list as many functions or effects of light as they can think of, and then

share the answers with the group. Discuss how these effects and functions are metaphors for our lives.

3. Discuss with your group whether or not anyone noticed the different lighting. How did the change in lighting change the feel or tone of the group?

5. HOMEWORK (CUE CARD)

Before concluding, encourage each person in the group to do the following before your next meeting:

- Find one thing in your life that you don't typically think of as spiritual. Invite the Holy Spirit to show you how it is worship to Him or expresses who He is. Ask for wisdom and creativity to demonstrate excellence in that area.
- If you have a copy of the book *Christ in You*, read chapter 5 to prepare for the next session.

6. PRAYER (CUE CARD)

Pray this over the group:

Lord, we pray as David prayed: God, be merciful to us and bless us. Cause Your face to shine upon us, that Your way may be known on the earth, Your salvation among all the nations.

Let every aspect of our lives be worship to You and ministry to the people around us. Give us the wisdom and creativity to live and work with excellence. May we face every problem with the conviction that the light within us is greater than any darkness. Amen.

SESSION 4
CONFIDENCE

One thing all great people have in common is that they would pay any price for what they believe in. No comfort in the world is enticing enough to pull them away from their convictions. No earthly possession has the power to keep them from pursuing the impossible. In many ways, they become possessed and obsessed with whatever it is they believe in. This character trait is essential for anyone who desires to affect the course of human history. If our convictions do not fully possess us, then at some point when the pressure is too much or the critics are too loud or the pain is too unbearable, we will retract.

Christ in You, page 93

PREPARE

Watch Video & Review Notes

(This time includes the Session 4 video and the notes that follow.)

1. CONFIDENCE

- "On this journey of learning who Jesus is in me, I find myself being more confident than I used to be and realizing I have a lot more to give. I have a lot more passion than I used to have. I think confidence comes from conviction. Once you have a conviction in something, you just become sold on it."

- "One of the reasons it's hard for Christians to step forward in confidence is that they are afraid of coming across as arrogant or prideful. There is a difference between confidence and arrogance. If you are at a distance, you can see one person walking in confidence and one in arrogance and they are going to look almost the same. But confidence is more motivated by what it can give and arrogance is more driven by what it can gain. As believers, we should be motivated by what we can give and move in confidence."

2. GREATNESS

- "The religious community hated Jesus. Another group of people hung out with Jesus and walked away thinking they were the greatest. These disciples argued about who was the greatest and asked Jesus who is the greatest. What is fascinating is that Jesus never rebukes them once. He never says, 'Knock it off,' or that it is bad. He actually encourages them in it."

- "Jesus says, 'That desire to be great—I gave that to you. But the way you are going about it is not the way we do it. The way we do it is to be like a child. If you are like a child, you will be the greatest in the Kingdom.' Jesus endorses a lifestyle of greatness and confidence, lives it and gives it a stamp of approval."

- "The Body of Christ is more scared of pride and arrogance than Jesus ever was. We just freak out when someone is operating in pride. Jesus never freaked out. He said, 'Go over here. That is how you become great.'"

3. FALSE HUMILITY

- "Most, if not all, false humility stems from fear of man. We care more about what others think than anything else. If I am about to do something and I go through a list, *What will this person and that person think?*, then I am going to be in false humility to make sure that I don't come across wrong. I am going to play that role instead of actually stepping into what God designed me to do."

- "We aren't designed to be slaves to fear. If we can recognize that a lot of that false humility stems from fear of man, then people are going to realize they have enslaved themselves to man's opinion rather than actually stepping into a place of confidence. Then we have to create a culture where it is accepted for someone to step out in confidence, where we're not like, 'You need to get back,' but where we actually encourage them to go farther."

- "If you look at the life of the disciples, there's not that much that Jesus rebuked them for. He just steered them. If they got off track, He would steer them over here. These eleven men ultimately—with Jesus—changed history because they lived with such confidence to see it happen. I am excited to see us stepping into that confidence."

4. NOTHING WITHOUT HIM; EVERYTHING WITH HIM

- "We have to remember we are nothing without Jesus. If you slice anything in existence right now, you will find Jesus in the center of it. That is what

Paul talks about in Colossians 1:15–17. He said everything in the universe was made by Him, through Him, for Him, and in Him. So we have to realize that we're nothing without Him, but we're actually everything with Him."

- "I think we have the potential to be the most arrogant people on the face of the earth if we only live with one side of the coin, that we are everything with Him. It's a tension I like to hold that we are nothing without Him, but everything with Him. I think if we hold those two really close, we will avoid becoming arrogant and prideful."

ADDITIONAL NOTES:

_____

_____

_____

_____

_____

_____

_____

_____

THINK & WRITE

"Session 4: Confidence" explores one of the clearest pieces of evidence that we have truly come to believe that Christ is in us and we are in Him—not as an idea that we assent to, but as a deep conviction and reality that we experience. The fruit of this conviction is confidence in who we are and what we have to offer the world through Christ. While many in the Church have been trained to resist the idea that they have greatness inside them or the potential to be great, Jesus actually inspired those around Him to be confident in who He said they were and what He said they could do through Him. This session challenges us to confront the obstacles in our thinking and church culture that don't align with Jesus' approach to inspiring and directing confidence in us. Eric covers this in chapter 5 of the book, which you will want to read before leading your group. This session raises the following questions:

- What does our level of confidence say about our level of conviction in who we are in Christ?
- Can you discern the difference between confidence and arrogance?

- Why should walking with Jesus inspire us to be great?

- How can we recognize when the fear of pride and fear of man are driving our thinking and behavior more than the desire to please God and serve others?

- How do we create a culture that approves of and trains people in confidence and true greatness?

- How do we hold on to the truth that we are nothing without Christ, and everything with Him?

Before leading Session 4, spend some time meditating on these questions. Write down two or three thoughts, experiences and insights from your life that you can share with the group.

_____

_____

_____

_____

_____

_____

_____

_____

WHAT YOU WILL NEED

- Session 4 video
- Pens and paper if you choose to do Activity 1

LEAD

1. WELCOME & KEY VERSE (SEE CUE CARD)

Read (or have someone in the group read) the Key Verse:

At that time the disciples came to Jesus, saying, "Who then is greatest in the kingdom of heaven?"
Then Jesus called a little child to Him, set him in the midst of them, and said, "Assuredly, I say to you, unless you are converted and become as little children, you will by no means enter the kingdom of heaven. Therefore whoever humbles himself as this little child is the greatest in the kingdom of heaven. Whoever receives one little child like this in My name receives Me."

Matthew 18:1–5

Ask the group, "What sticks out to you in these verses? How do they apply to your life?" Allow two or three people to respond.

2. SESSION VIDEO

- Watch the Session 4 video.

3. CONVERSATION (CUE CARD)

Share one or two thoughts from your preparation work, and then discuss the following:

- Discuss a time in your life when you experienced a crisis or a trial. Were you shaken, or were you confident in God? What truth did you hold on to during that time? Or what truth would have helped you get through the situation?

- How do we overcome the fear of man and cultivate an unshakable desire to believe, obey and please God above all others?

- In *Christ in You*, Eric writes, "I believe the reason Jesus did not spend a whole lot of time rebuking His disciples as they were dealing with pride and elitism was that He was living life with them and teaching them along the way. This is essential for us to understand and live out. The dominant context of the disciples' lives is that they were in covenant and in community with Jesus and each other. That is how they were able to grow and do things that changed history. Jesus modeled it for them by leading the way" (page 140).

- How do we build communities where people grow in confidence and see that true greatness looks like serving God and others?

4. ACTIVITY (CUE CARD)

Do one or both of these activities with your group:

1. Give everyone a piece of paper and have them finish this sentence: "I am great at . . ." Have one person collect the pieces of paper and read each answer out loud. As the person reads each answer, have the group guess who wrote it.

2. Ask two or three people in the group to share briefly about a person they know who demonstrates true confidence and greatness through Christ.

5. HOMEWORK (CUE CARD)

Before concluding, encourage each person in the group to do the following before your next meeting:

- Find some information on a historical person who interests you. What made this person great? How did he or she change history? How did this

33

person handle conflict and crises? What can you learn from his or her life to apply to yours?

- If you have a copy of the book *Christ in You*, read chapters 6 and 7 to prepare for the next session.

6. PRAYER (CUE CARD)

Pray this over the group:

Father, we know that without faith, it is impossible to please You. Free us forever of all man-pleasing efforts and the fear of man. Cause our hearts to burn with the conviction of who You are in us and who we are in You. Give us unshakable confidence to offer what You have put inside us to the world around us. Increase our ability to serve well and honor the greatness in one another. May we never forget that we are nothing without You, and everything with You. Amen.

SESSION 5
TRUST

A true friend is willing to become a slave for another friend, and a true friend will become a servant in a heartbeat. Being a friend of God means you are willing to offer yourself as a slave and a servant. I know that when you begin to live this out, you will begin to realize that the trust between you and God goes both ways. God really does trust you more than you realize.

Christ in You, page 124

PREPARE

Watch Video & Review Notes

(This time includes the Session 5 video and the notes that follow.)

1. CO-LABORING: A TWO-WAY RELATIONSHIP

- "Most believers believe that we co-labor with God. But a true co-laboring relationship, as in any true relationship, is really two-way. It doesn't mean we are God and He isn't. He is always God. But it means He is actually intrigued by us and by what we have to bring to the table."

- "If my two daughters spend the rest of their lives only serving or asking or doing what I want, then I have failed as a father. Our goal as fathers is to raise up children that are able to dream big and take on challenges. That doesn't come through a one-way relationship. That comes through co-laboring, partnering together and trusting."

- "In her younger years, my daughter Selah would come home from school and tell her mom she needed a costume for a costume party at school the next day. She always wanted some elaborate costume, so Candace would have to get the sewing machine and fabrics out late at night and stay up late making this elaborate costume. It was this beautiful picture of Candace partnering with Selah to accomplish Selah's idea. Parents do crazy things for their kids. That is our natural response to our children—to help them. God very much wants that kind of relationship with us as well. He actually wants to know what you think."

2. DREAM AGAIN, DREAM BIG

- "How can we move into dreaming big? Start finding out what you are passionate about. . . . What is important to you? What are you actually excited about? You will find out in time that God is very passionate about that thing. He is your number-one fan in that passion you have."

- One trait of a healthy family is that the kids dream. When the kids feel the liberty to dream and do crazy things, it is because their family has a culture and an environment where they have permission and it doesn't end. I love running into families with teenagers who are just dreaming about life. That is normal for young kids."

3. WHEN GOD LETS YOU DECIDE

- "Candace and I got to a point where we had to make a major decision. We had four beautiful opportunities in front of us and needed to know what to do. We did the normal prayer, fasting, asking everyone, but we noticed God never said one word. After a few months, I felt as though God spoke to me and said, *I will honor whatever decision you make.* It was one of the most profound, life-changing moments. I realized I had entered a dimension of relationship with Him where it was a friendship as well."

- "Prior to that decision, my approach was, *You tell me what to do and I'm on it.* I think that is the easiest level of obedience. When He says, *I will honor whatever decision you make,* it is an expression of trust. Then I realized that if God makes every decision for us, then at the end of our life we'd have nothing to give an account for. There has to be freedom and trust from Him to choose to live our lives."

- "Most believers think every decision is either right or wrong, so we approach it with, *I just don't want to make the wrong decision.* We are constantly looking for the wrong one. I think there are decisions in life where there are no wrong choices. They're all right. The question is, what do you want to do? When we are talking about morality, obviously that's a different conversation. But God actually trusts us to make decisions."

4. FEAR OF FAILURE

- "The last thing you want to do is fail. But I think it's important to realize that God is going to make everything work for good. So if we do fail at something that He trusted us in, the beautiful thing is that if we stick to it, He is going to use it to His benefit and our benefit. Failure is something we hate to do, but boy, is it beneficial. Am I glad I failed? No. But I grew up. I learned a lot after that."

- "When you live in a relationship where you are the child of a good Dad, your failure doesn't bring shame and guilt. Your failure brings you closer to Him, or actually, brings Him closer to you. When you don't realize you are the child of a good Dad—when you come from a different setting where when you failed, you got blasted by your father or whoever the authority was—you connect failure with shame and guilt. But failure in the Kingdom is different."

5. REPRESENTING HIM

- "Why would God put Christ in you if He didn't trust you? Some people will say, 'To save you.' That is one reason He is in you. But we have to ask another question when we move from just 'getting into heaven' into 'Kingdom coming on earth.' When we start to move into that theology, we begin to realize that the most valuable Person ever has been given to live inside us."

- "You and I represent Jesus everywhere we go. God is trusting that we do that, so He gives us power, authority and light. That is a massive sign of trust. . . . You are going to be the only Jesus people see. That is like me putting my business logo on you and saying, 'Okay, everywhere you go, you're going to tell people about my business. If you do a really bad job at it, it's going to put a bad light on my business.' He actually trusts that we will do it well. We know through history and through modern times it isn't always done well. But He trusts us and put Jesus in us—for eternity purposes and for now."

ADDITIONAL NOTES:

_____

_____

_____

_____

_____

_____

_____

_____

_____

THINK & WRITE

"Session 5: Trust" explores the idea that God intends to have a mutual relationship and partnership with us. The One who first created and then saved us wants us to bring our full personhood to the table as we co-labor with Him. He cares about our dreams and desires—He put them in us! He cares about our free will to make decisions. There is no love without free choice. He is not afraid of our failures or mistakes; these are some of the best moments in which He can draw close to us and teach us. And He is not ashamed to put His reputation on the line by calling us His friends and family members. Eric covers this in chapter 6 of the book, which you will want to read before leading your group. (Also read chapter 7.) This session raises the following questions:

- Do we really believe that our loving Father wants us to dream big with Him?
- Do we value our passions and dreams the way God does?
- How would we do things differently if we believed God trusted us to make good decisions?
- How strong is our fear of failure, and what does this tell us about how free we are from guilt and shame?
- How would we live differently if we were not afraid of failure?

Before leading Session 5, spend some time meditating on these questions. Write down two or three thoughts, experiences and insights from your life that you can share with the group.

_____

_____

_____

_____

_____

_____

_____

_____

WHAT YOU WILL NEED

- Session 5 video
- Pens and paper if you choose to do Activity 1

- A display of Activity 2's declaration (or a printed copy for each participant) if you will be reading it aloud together as a group

LEAD

1. WELCOME & KEY VERSE (SEE CUE CARD)

Read (or have someone in the group read) the Key Verse twice:

To them God willed to make known what are the riches of the glory of this mystery among the Gentiles: which is Christ in you, the hope of glory.

Colossians 1:27

Ask the group, "What sticks out to you in this verse? How does it apply to your life?" Allow two or three people to respond.

2. SESSION VIDEO

Watch the Session 5 video.

3. CONVERSATION (CUE CARD)

Share one or two thoughts from your preparation work, and then discuss the following:

- In *Christ in You*, Eric writes, "It is important that we do not think our relationship with God started from the premise of His distrusting us. It is important that we do not think it is our responsibility to spend the rest of our life earning God's trust" (page 109). Do you think you live with the sense that you have to earn God's trust? How does it change things to realize that His trust is not based on you, but on Himself and Him in you?

- What are you the most passionate about? What dream would you love to co-labor with God to see realized?

- How has the fear of failure influenced you in the past? How does it influence our perception of other people's failures? How can we contribute to an environment where people are not afraid to fail?

4. ACTIVITY (CUE CARD)

Do one or both of these activities with your group:

1. Start a dream list. Have everyone write down 10 dreams they have in their hearts.
2. Read the following declaration aloud together as a group (from a display or printed copies):

39

My Father trusts me because He made me and lives in me. He loves the dreams in my heart. He believes in my ability to make good decisions. I am not afraid to dream big. I am not afraid to take risks. I am not afraid to fail. I represent my Father wherever I go.

5. HOMEWORK (CUE CARD)

Before concluding, encourage each person in the group to do the following before your next meeting:

- Get your dream list up to 20 dreams.
- Ask the Father to highlight one of these dreams. Do one thing that feels risky to go after it.
- If you have a copy of the book *Christ in You*, read chapters 8 and 9 to prepare for the next session.

6. PRAYER (CUE CARD)

Pray this over the group:

Father, it is truly awesome that You chose to put Christ, the hope of glory, inside us. We pray that this truth would forever free us from small thinking and the fear of failure. Help us to trust You as You trust us, and to be confident in Your total commitment to seeing Christ fully formed in us. Help us dream with You and take wild risks with You. We want to grow up and show the world who our Daddy is. Amen.

SESSION 6
FREEDOM

When you and I learn to let God direct our paths, it does not give us permission to lie around and wait for God to do everything. It is about being diligent in everything we do and letting God promote us and open up doors that only He can open.

Christ in You, page 157

PREPARE

Watch Video & Review Notes

(This time includes the Session 6 video and the notes that follow.)

1. FIVE TRUTHS FOR FREEDOM

- "There are five truths that will help people begin to move in freedom. The first one is that *perfect love casts out fear*. Sometimes we spend a lot of time trying to get rid of fear when the best way is to experience perfect love. Perfect love can only come from God Himself, so put yourself in a place to experience the perfect love of God, and it will remove all fear."

- "The second thing is that *truth alone can expose lies*. Anytime we come upon truth, it exposes what isn't truth. It is important for us to constantly be on this pursuit of truth."

- "The third thing is to *build the wall that is in front of you*. This is probably the hardest of all of them because it is the boring one. It comes from the story of Nehemiah commanding the people in the city to build the wall in front of them. Jesus touches on that in the parable of the talents and stewardship—the value of what is in front of you. That is all you need to focus on right now. Sometimes I think we're so vision-oriented that we don't live in the day and in the moment."

- "The fourth one I love. *God is a good teacher*—He is the best teacher, period. A good teacher always prepares you for the test. In Philippians, Paul talks about how God began a good work in you (and will be faithful to complete it). Success is not just me getting somewhere; it is how I do the journey, and knowing that God is teaching me as I go. There is so much freedom and liberty in that, rather than, *I'm failing, I'm failing. . . . I've finally arrived*, it's *I'm getting better, I'm becoming more successful, God will teach me*. Success is being faithful on the journey, realizing that God is a good teacher."

- "The fifth truth is that *self-promotion is the absence of trust in God*. Self-promotion is, *I don't trust God enough that He has it taken care of, so I am going to do it myself*. If we fully trust in God, our need to self-promote is nearly nonexistent. What is the difference between striving and being diligent? They can look very much the same. My answer is to ask, 'Can you tell when you are striving?' I have never had someone say they can't tell. So I say, 'Then that is where you need to stop and not push anymore. Be diligent, but when you know you are starting to strive, lay off, pull back and stop right there.'"

2. THE FULLNESS OF GOD

- "Colossians 1:19 says that it pleased the Father that in Him all the fullness would dwell. The fullness of God is something we do not have the ability to comprehend or grasp. The fullness of God means there is no end. Isaiah 9:7 says that the increase of His government will have no end. The word for 'no end' actually means the end doesn't exist. Somehow that fullness lives in Jesus."

- "Then in Colossians 1:27, Paul reveals the greatest mystery ever: 'Christ in you, the hope of glory.' The fullness of God lives in His Son, who lives in us. So I can confidently say that the fullness is living in us."

- "I believe that the Body of Christ is experiencing more of God than they did five hundred years ago. We know we're stepping more and more into the fullness. My final charge in this whole thing would be, let's spend the rest of our life hungry for the fullness of God. Let's spend the rest of our life finding out what is in us and in the people around us. . . . I want to give my life to experiencing, demonstrating, activating and living in the fullness and living from the fullness of God."

ADDITIONAL NOTES:

_____

_____

_____

_____

_____

_____

_____

_____

THINK & WRITE

"Session 6: Freedom" presents some crucial guidelines for "living with a green light"—building a lifestyle of freedom where we are running fearlessly after God and His purpose for our lives. First and foremost, we must continuously pursue increase in encountering God's love and knowing His truth, as these neutralize and destroy fear and lies. Second, we must check in often to make sure we are demonstrating trust in God by faithfully stewarding what He has entrusted to us, expecting Him to prepare us for what we will need in the future, and maintaining rest and diligence without striving. Third, we need to keep framing our journey in the context of God's endless Kingdom and unfathomable fullness, which fuels us with ever-renewing hope and vision for what lies ahead. Eric covers this in chapter 8 of the book, which you will want to read before leading your group. (Also read chapter 9.) This session raises the following questions:

- What are some strategies for going after deeper encounters with love and truth in the face of fear?
- Where are we struggling to "build the wall in front of us"? How might this be connected to a lack of trust in God?
- What are some strategies for cultivating focus on the present and trusting that we are just where we are supposed to be in life?
- Are we trusting God to get us ready for the future and promote us at the right time?
- How do we live with a greater awareness of the fullness of God in us?

Before leading Session 6, spend some time meditating on these questions. Write down two or three thoughts, experiences and insights from your life that you can share with the group.

_____

_____

_____

43

_____

_____

_____

_____

_____

_____

WHAT YOU WILL NEED

- Session 6 video
- Two or three sets of blocks if you choose to do Activity 1

LEAD

1. WELCOME & KEY VERSE (SEE CUE CARD)

Read (or have someone in the group read) the Key Verse twice:

For it pleased the Father that in Him [Christ] all the fullness should dwell, and by Him to reconcile all things to Himself, by Him, whether things on earth or things in heaven, having made peace through the blood of His cross.

Colossians 1:19–20

Ask the group, "What sticks out to you in these verses? How do they apply to your life?" Allow two or three people to respond.

2. SESSION VIDEO

Watch the Session 6 video.

3. CONVERSATION (CUE CARD)

Share one or two thoughts from your preparation work, and then discuss the following:

- Where are you experiencing fear in your life? What lie are you believing that fuels that fear? What is the truth that God says about that fear?
- In *Christ in You*, Eric writes, "Commonly, what is right in front of us is the last thing we want to do or want to give our time to. There is always greener grass somewhere else or something that seems way more appealing. One of the greatest privileges in life, though, is to convert a field of weeds into one that is full of green grass. The mandate of every believer is to step into a dire situation and see it turn around" (page 152). What

is the "wall" or "field" in front of you? How do you think God wants to partner with you to bring restoration there?

- "God is a good teacher." What is He teaching you in this season of your life?

4. ACTIVITY (CUE CARD)

Do one or both of these activities with your group:

1. Give two or three people in the group a set of blocks and instruct them to build a wall separately from the others. Have the rest of the group observe what they are doing as they build. How are they being strategic with their pieces? Are they looking at their neighbor's wall? If so, is it to compare or to learn? After the walls are finished, invite your group participants to share their observations.

2. Spend some time worshiping as a group. Invite the Holy Spirit to encounter the group with love and truth, break off fear and lies and increase freedom. "Where the Spirit of the Lord is, there is freedom" (2 Corinthians 3:17 ESV).

5. HOMEWORK (CUE CARD)

Before concluding, encourage your group participants to remember that this *Christ in You* study was just the beginning of their journey toward experiencing the fullness of Christ in them. In concluding this final session, invite each person to share one key thing he or she has learned and will be taking away from this study. Ask your participants what kind of goals they will set for applying what they have learned from *Christ in You* to their lives.

6. PRAYER (CUE CARD)

Pray this over the group:

Father, thank You for all You have done in us throughout these weeks together. There is no greater privilege and joy than to live in Your Kingdom, where there is no end to the increase of Your love, truth, power and freedom in our lives. Keep coming and drawing us into Your fullness, so that Christ in us displaces all fear, mistrust and striving. We love You!

Eric Johnson co-leads Bethel Redding alongside his wife, Candace. He is a sixth-generation minister who began his ministry career as a youth pastor in Weaverville, California. In addition to writing *Christ in You*, Eric co-authored the book *Momentum: What God Starts Never Ends* with his father, Bill Johnson. Eric has a passion to see transformation take place in the lives of people, cities and nations. Besides spending time with his wife and two daughters, Eric enjoys the outdoors.

You can learn more about Eric and his ministry and keep up with him on the following:

ibethel.org and bethelredding.com

Instagram: @ericj76

Twitter: @ericbj

www.facebook.com/ericbryantjohnson

KEY VERSE

Leader cue: "This is the Key Verse for this week." *Read (or have someone read) the verse aloud twice.* Ask the group, "What sticks out to you in these verses? How do they apply to your life?" Allow two or three people to respond.

But the natural man does not receive the things of the Spirit of God, for they are foolishness to him; nor can he know them, because they are spiritually discerned. But he who is spiritual judges all things, yet he himself is rightly judged by no one. For "who has known the mind of the Lord that he may instruct Him?" But we have the mind of Christ.

1 Corinthians 2:14–16

Mindsets

CONVERSATION

Share one or two thoughts from your preparation work, and then discuss the following:

- What does it mean to think of yourself as the child of a really good Dad? Do we really think about ourselves the way God thinks about us?
- In his introduction to *Christ in You*, Eric writes, "For centuries, the Church has largely focused on salvation. The main thrust has been to get people saved so they could go to heaven. What is interesting is that while the Church has spent most of its time talking about going to heaven, Jesus spent quite a bit of His time talking about bringing the Kingdom of heaven to earth" (page 20). What are the implications of shifting from a "getting saved and going to heaven" mindset to an "expressing salvation now and bringing heaven to earth" mindset?
- What are some ways that we express our salvation and/or see the Kingdom coming as a present reality in our daily lives?
- How do you want the six sessions in this study to change your perception of God? What else do you want to get out of these sessions?

Mindsets

ACTIVITY

Do one or both of these activities with your group:

1. Word/phrase associations to check your beliefs. Read the following phrases to the group. Have participants write down their first reaction. Then discuss their answers. Ask, "Which phrases didn't feel true?"
   - "God is good."
   - "God trusts you."
   - "You are a saint."
   - "Jesus lives in you."
   - "You were created for great things."
2. Take time to "pull out the gold" in each other. Break up into groups of two or three and encourage each other. Before you speak out, ask God who each person is and what he or she was born for.

HOMEWORK

Before concluding, encourage each person in the group to do the following before your next meeting:

- Meditate on 1 Corinthians 2:14–16 throughout the week.
- Ask God what mindset or perceptions He wants to change in you.
- Choose your favorite painting and bring along a print of it next time. Do a little research on the painting so you can tell the group the story behind it. (Leader: Assign this only if the group will be doing Activity 3 next time.)
- If you have a copy of the book *Christ in You*, read the Introduction and chapters 1 and 2 to prepare for the next session.

PRAYER

Pray this over the group:

Father, we thank You that we are the sons and daughters of a really good Dad. Teach us how to see ourselves the way You see us. Show us what it means to express our salvation in every area of life.

Jesus, we want to see the world the way You see it. Give us the heart of a child to believe that "Christ in us" means we can go higher and further than we can imagine. Let us become like the One who lives in us and fall in love with You more than ever before. Amen.

CHRIST IN YOU

KEY VERSE

Leader cue: "This is the Key Verse for this week." *Read (or have someone read) the verse aloud twice.* Ask the group, "What sticks out to you in these verses? How do they apply to your life?" Allow two or three people to respond.

Then God said, "Let Us make man in Our image, according to Our likeness; let them have dominion over the fish of the sea, over the birds of the air, and over the cattle, over all the earth and over every creeping thing that creeps on the earth." So God created man in His own image; in the image of God He created him; male and female He created them. Then God blessed them, and God said to them, "Be fruitful and multiply; fill the earth and subdue it; have dominion over the fish of the sea, over the birds of the air, and over every living thing that moves on the earth."

And God said, "See, I have given you every herb that yields seed which is on the face of all the earth, and every tree whose fruit yields seed; to you it shall be for food. Also, to every beast of the earth, to every bird of the air, and to everything that creeps on the earth, in which there is life, I have given every green herb for food"; and it was so. Then God saw everything that He had made, and indeed it was very good. So the evening and the morning were the sixth day.

Genesis 1:26–31

CHRIST IN YOU

CONVERSATION

Share one or two thoughts from your preparation work, and then discuss the following:

- How can we tell if our hearts are getting harder and more calloused toward people, or are becoming more compassionate?
- Think of some people you find difficult to love. What does God say about these people (or their group, if applicable)?
- In *Christ in You*, Eric writes, "If we are going to navigate the sin and evil rampant on the earth and help usher the Kingdom into every level of society, we have to recognize how important it is to see the image of God in every person we meet. If we do not realize the importance of that image in them, we most likely will deal with sin and evil from the basis of a short-term mindset that has as its goal alleviating the consequences of sin but not helping the person become healthy and whole as well as saved.

  "I believe that if we as believers have a good grasp of seeing the image of God in people, then we will cultivate a deep love for them that does not have an agenda attached. People will not become the objects of our agenda. Rather, we will see the uniqueness of each person, and we will spend our lives simply loving people into the Kingdom. That all by itself is bound to have an eternal effect on our churches, government and society" (pages 33–34).

  What does it mean to deal with sin with a short-term mindset? What does it mean to love people without having an agenda?

CHRIST IN YOU

ACTIVITY

Do any of these activities with your group:

1. Invite someone you would not normally have a meal with to lunch—maybe a sports team coach, a homeless person, a business owner, a neighbor or a pastor. Ask the person, "What's your story?" Show real interest and aim to see who he or she is as a person.
2. Volunteer as a group to help a neighbor or someone in your church. (Ideas: Rake leaves, help a family move, cook dinner for an older couple, etc.)
3. Have everyone talk for a few minutes about the print they brought of their favorite painting, on which they have done a little research so they can share the story behind it.

HOMEWORK

Before concluding, encourage each person in the group to do the following before your next meeting:

- Pick someone you know or some high-profile person (a celebrity, politician, CEO, etc.) whom you frequently criticize or have a hard time loving. Give God permission to talk to you about your attitude toward that person. Ask Him to change your heart and attitude.
- Bring your favorite gadget or invention with you to the next group session, or a picture of it if the item is too big. (Leader: Assign this only if the group will be doing Activity 1 next time.)
- If you have a copy of the book *Christ in You*, read chapters 3 and 4 to prepare for the next session.

PRAYER

Pray this over the group:

Father, You made us in Your image. Then You became one of us, died for us and rose again as the image of redeemed humanity. As we look at ourselves and those around us, let us see Your image, Your value and Your love more clearly than anything else. Encounter us with Your goodness, so we can show that goodness to a world full of people whom You love. Amen.

CHRIST IN YOU

KEY VERSE

Leader cue: "This is the Key Verse for this week." *Read (or have someone read) the verse aloud twice.* Ask the group, "What sticks out to you in these verses? How do they apply to your life?" Allow two or three people to respond.

The LORD possessed me at the beginning of His way, before His works of old. I have been established from everlasting, from the beginning, before there was ever an earth. When there were no depths I was brought forth, when there were no fountains abounding with water. Before the mountains were settled, before the hills, I was brought forth; while as yet He had not made the earth or the fields, or the primal dust of the world. When He prepared the heavens, I was there, when He drew a circle on the face of the deep, when He established the clouds above, when He strengthened the fountains of the deep, when He assigned to the sea its limit, so that the waters would not transgress His command, when He marked out the foundations of the earth, then I was beside Him as a master craftsman; and I was daily His delight, rejoicing always before Him, rejoicing in His inhabited world, and my delight was with the sons of men.

Proverbs 8:22–31

CHRIST IN YOU

CONVERSATION

Share one or two thoughts from your preparation work, and then discuss the following:

- In *Christ in You*, Eric writes, "David tapped into the heart of God and realized that God wants to bless us abundantly in every area of our lives, to the point that the nations take notice. I believe one of the ways for believers to disciple the nations is to walk out the favor and abundance that God shines in and on our lives" (page 61). Do you feel as if you have tapped in to the heart of God in this way? Why or why not?

- What is spiritual? Are there areas of your life you have viewed as non-spiritual? How would you approach such an area differently if you saw it as worship to God and ministry to others?

- What are some examples of what it looks like to take something of no value and make it of value through the wisdom and creativity of God?

ACTIVITY

Do any of these activities with your group:

1. Wisdom is not just good advice; it is creativity and problem-solving. Have everyone talk about the gadget or invention they brought. How did it change or improve their lives? How would their lives be different without it? How does this express wisdom?

2. Do another word association exercise with the word *light*. Have everyone list as many functions or effects of light as they can think of, and then share the answers with the group. Discuss how these effects and functions are metaphors for our lives.

3. Discuss with your group whether or not anyone noticed the different lighting. How did the change in lighting change the feel or tone of the group?

HOMEWORK

Before concluding, encourage each person in the group to do the following before your next meeting:

- Find one thing in your life that you don't typically think of as spiritual. Invite the Holy Spirit to show you how it is worship to Him or expresses who He is. Ask for wisdom and creativity to demonstrate excellence in that area.

- If you have a copy of the book *Christ in You*, read chapter 5 to prepare for the next session.

PRAYER

Pray this over the group:

Lord, we pray as David prayed: God, be merciful to us and bless us. Cause Your face to shine upon us, that Your way may be known on the earth, Your salvation among all the nations.

Let every aspect of our lives be worship to You and ministry to the people around us. Give us the wisdom and creativity to live and work with excellence. May we face every problem with the conviction that the light within us is greater than any darkness. Amen.

Light

CHRIST IN YOU

KEY VERSE

Leader cue: "This is the Key Verse for this week." *Read (or have someone read) the verse aloud twice.* Ask the group, "What sticks out to you in these verses? How do they apply to your life?" Allow two or three people to respond.

At that time the disciples came to Jesus, saying, "Who then is greatest in the kingdom of heaven?"

Then Jesus called a little child to Him, set him in the midst of them, and said, "Assuredly, I say to you, unless you are converted and become as little children, you will by no means enter the kingdom of heaven. Therefore whoever humbles himself as this little child is the greatest in the kingdom of heaven. Whoever receives one little child like this in My name receives Me."

Matthew 18:1–5

Confidence

CONVERSATION

Share one or two thoughts from your preparation work, and then discuss the following:

- Discuss a time in your life when you experienced a crisis or trial. Were you shaken, or were you confident in God? What truth did you hold on to during that time? Or what truth would have helped you get through the situation?

- How do we overcome the fear of man and cultivate an unshakable desire to believe, obey and please God above all others?

- In *Christ in You*, Eric writes, "I believe the reason Jesus did not spend a whole lot of time rebuking His disciples as they were dealing with pride and elitism was that He was living life with them and teaching them along the way. This is essential for us to understand and live out. The dominant context of the disciples' lives is that they were in covenant and in community with Jesus and each other. That is how they were able to grow and do things that changed history. Jesus modeled it for them by leading the way" (page 140). How do we build communities where people grow in confidence and see that true greatness looks like serving God and others?

ACTIVITY

Do one or both of these activities with your group:

1. Give everyone a piece of paper and have them finish this sentence: "I am great at . . ." Have one person collect the pieces of paper and read each answer out loud. As the person reads each answer, have the group guess who wrote it.

2. Ask two or three people in the group to share briefly about a person they know who demonstrates true confidence and greatness through Christ.

CHRIST IN YOU

HOMEWORK

Before concluding, encourage each person in the group to do the following before your next meeting:

- Find some information on a historical person who interests you. What made this person great? How did he or she change history? How did this person handle conflict and crises? What can you learn from his or her life to apply to yours?
- If you have a copy of the book *Christ in You*, read chapters 6 and 7 to prepare for the next session.

CHRIST IN YOU

PRAYER

Pray this over the group:

Father, we know that without faith, it is impossible to please You. Free us forever of all man-pleasing efforts and the fear of man. Cause our hearts to burn with the conviction of who You are in us and who we are in You. Give us unshakable confidence to offer what You have put inside us to the world around us. Increase our ability to serve well and honor the greatness in one another. May we never forget that we are nothing without You, and everything with You. Amen.

CHRIST IN YOU

KEY VERSE

Leader cue: "This is the Key Verse for this week." *Read (or have someone read) the verse aloud twice.* Ask the group, "What sticks out to you in this verse? How does it apply to your life?" Allow two or three people to respond.

To them God willed to make known what are the riches of the glory of this mystery among the Gentiles: which is Christ in you, the hope of glory.

Colossians 1:27

CHRIST IN YOU

CONVERSATION

Share one or two thoughts from your preparation work, and then discuss the following:

- In *Christ in You*, Eric writes, "It is important that we do not think our relationship with God started from the premise of His distrusting us. It is important that we do not think it is our responsibility to spend the rest of our life earning God's trust" (page 109). Do you think you live with the sense that you have to earn God's trust? How does it change things to realize that His trust is not based on you, but on Himself and Him in you?

- What are you the most passionate about? What dream would you love to co-labor with God to see realized?

- How has the fear of failure influenced you in the past? How does it influence our perception of other people's failures? How can we contribute to an environment where people are not afraid to fail?

ACTIVITY

Do one or both of these activities with your group:

1. Start a dream list. Have everyone write down 10 dreams they have in their hearts.
2. Read the following declaration aloud together as a group (from a display or printed copies):

My Father trusts me because He made me and lives in me. He loves the dreams in my heart. He believes in my ability to make good decisions. I am not afraid to dream big. I am not afraid to take risks. I am not afraid to fail. I represent my Father wherever I go.

HOMEWORK

Before concluding, encourage each person in the group to do the following before your next meeting:

- Get your dream list up to 20 dreams.
- Ask the Father to highlight one of these dreams. Do one thing that feels risky to go after it.
- If you have a copy of the book *Christ in You*, read chapters 8 and 9 to prepare for the next session.

Trust

PRAYER

Pray this over the group:

Father, it is truly awesome that You chose to put Christ, the hope of glory, inside us. We pray that this truth would forever free us from small thinking and the fear of failure. Help us to trust You as You trust us, and to be confident in Your total commitment to seeing Christ fully formed in us. Help us dream with You and take wild risks with You. We want to grow up and show the world who our Daddy is. Amen.

Freedom

KEY VERSE

Leader cue: "This is the Key Verse for this week." *Read (or have someone read) the verse aloud twice.* Ask the group, "What sticks out to you in these verses? How do they apply to your life?" Allow two or three people to respond.

For it pleased the Father that in Him [Christ] all the fullness should dwell, and by Him to reconcile all things to Himself, by Him, whether things on earth or things in heaven, having made peace through the blood of His cross.

Colossians 1:19–20

CONVERSATION

Share one or two thoughts from your preparation work, and then discuss the following:

- Where are you experiencing fear in your life? What lie are you believing that fuels that fear? What is the truth that God says about that fear?

- In *Christ in You*, Eric writes, "Commonly, what is right in front of us is the last thing we want to do or want to give our time to. There is always greener grass somewhere else or something that seems way more appealing. One of the greatest privileges in life, though, is to convert a field of weeds into one that is full of green grass. The mandate of every believer is to step into a dire situation and see it turn around" (page 152). What is the "wall" or "field" in front of you? How do you think God wants to partner with you to bring restoration there?

- "God is a good teacher." What is He teaching you in this season of your life?

ACTIVITY

Do one or both of these activities with your group:

1. Give two or three people in the group a set of blocks and instruct them to build a wall separately from the others. Have the rest of the group observe what they are doing as they build. How are they being strategic with their pieces? Are they looking at their neighbor's wall? If so, is it to compare or to learn? After the walls are finished, invite your group participants to share their observations.

2. Spend some time worshiping as a group. Invite the Holy Spirit to encounter the group with love and truth, break off fear and lies and increase freedom. "Where the Spirit of the Lord is, there is freedom" (2 Corinthians 3:17 ESV).

HOMEWORK

Before concluding, encourage your group participants to remember that this *Christ in You* study was just the beginning of their journey toward experiencing the fullness of Christ in them. In concluding this final session, invite each person to share one key thing he or she has learned and will be taking away from this study. Ask your participants what kind of goals they will set for applying what they have learned from *Christ in You* to their lives.

PRAYER

Pray this over the group:

Father, thank You for all You have done in us throughout these weeks together. There is no greater privilege and joy than to live in Your Kingdom, where there is no end to the increase of Your love, truth, power and freedom in our lives. Keep coming and drawing us into Your fullness, so that Christ in us displaces all fear, mistrust and striving. We love You!